Life Lessons

from THE INSPIRED WORD of GOD

BOOK of ROMANS

MAX LUCADO

General Editor

Design and cover art—by Koechel Peterson and Associates, Inc., Minneapolis, Minnesota.

Produced with the assistance of the Livingstone Corporation.

ISBN: 08499-5249-2
Published by Word Publishing

TABLE OF CONTENTS

HOW TO STUDY THE BIBLE

BY MAX LUCADO

This is a peculiar book you are holding. Words crafted in another language. Deeds done in a distant era. Events recorded in a far-off land. Counsel offered to a foreign people. This is a peculiar book.

It's surprising that anyone reads it. It's too old. Some of its writings date back five thousand years. It's too bizarre. The book speaks of incredible floods, fires, earthquakes, and people with supernatural abilities. It's too radical. The Bible calls for undying devotion to a carpenter who called himself God's Son.

Logic says this book shouldn't survive. Too old, too bizarre, too radical.

The Bible has been banned, burned, scoffed, and ridiculed. Scholars have mocked it as foolish. Kings have branded it as illegal. A thousand times over it the grave has been dug and the dirge has begun, but somehow the Bible never stays in the grave. Not only has it survived, it has thrived. It is the single most popular book in all of history. It has been the best-selling book in the world for years!

There is no way on earth to explain it. Which perhaps is the only explanation. The answer? The Bible's durability is not found on earth; it is found in heaven. For the millions who have tested its claims and claimed its promises, there is but one answer—the Bible is God's book and God's voice.

As you read it, you would be wise to give some thought to two questions. What is the purpose of the Bible? and How do I study the Bible? Time spent reflecting on these two issues will greatly enhance your Bible study.

What is the purpose of the Bible?

Let the Bible itself answer that question.

Since you were a child you have known the Holy Scriptures which are able to make you wise. And that wisdom leads to salvation through faith in Christ Jesus.

(2 Tim. 3:15)

The purpose of the Bible? Salvation. God's highest passion is to get his children home. His book, the Bible, describes his plan of salvation. The purpose of the Bible is to proclaim God's plan and passion to save his children.

That is the reason this book has endured through the centuries. It dares to tackle the toughest questions about life: Where do I go after I die? Is there a God? What do I do with my fears? The Bible offers answers to these crucial questions. It is the treasure map that leads us to God's highest treasure, eternal life.

But how do we use the Bible? Countless copies of Scripture sit unread on bookshelves and nightstands simply because people don't know how to read it. What can we do to make the Bible real in our lives?

The clearest answer is found in the words of Jesus.

"Ask," he promised, *"and God will give it to you. Search and you will find. Knock, and the door will open for you."*

(Matt. 7:7)

The first step in understanding the Bible is asking God to help us. We should read prayerfully. If anyone understands God's Word, it is because of God and not the reader.

But the Helper will teach you everything and will cause you to remember all that I told you. The Helper is the Holy Spirit whom the Father will send in my name.

(John 14:24)

Before reading the Bible, pray. Invite God to speak to you. Don't go to Scripture looking for your idea, go searching for his.

Not only should we read the Bible prayerfully, we should read it carefully. *Search and you will find* is the pledge. The Bible is not a newspaper to be skimmed but rather a mine to be quarried. *Search for it like silver, and hunt for it like hidden treasure. Then you will understand respect for the Lord, and you will find that you know God* (Prov. 2:4).

Any worthy find requires effort. The Bible is no exception. To understand the Bible you don't have to be brilliant, but you must be willing to roll up your sleeves and search.

Be a worker who is not ashamed and who uses the true teaching in the right way.

(2 Tim. 2:15)

Here's a practical point. Study the Bible a bit at a time. Hunger is not satisfied by eating twenty-one meals in one sitting once a week. The body needs a steady diet to remain strong. So does the soul. When God sent food to his people in the wilderness, he didn't provide loaves already made. Instead, he sent them manna in the shape of *thin flakes, like frost . . . on the desert ground* (Exod. 16:14).

God gave manna in limited portions.

God sends spiritual food the same way. He opens the heavens with just enough nutrients for today's hunger. He provides, *a command here, a command there. A rule here, a rule there. A little lesson here, a little lesson there* (Isa. 28:10).

Don't be discouraged if your reading reaps a small harvest. Some days a lesser portion is all that is needed. What is important is to search every day for that day's message. A steady diet of God's Word over a lifetime builds a healthy soul and mind.

A little girl returned from her first day at school. Her mom asked, "Did you learn anything?" "Apparently not enough," the girl responded, "I have to go back tomorrow and the next day and the next. . . ."

Such is the case with learning. And such is the case with Bible study. Understanding comes little by little over a lifetime.

There is a third step in understanding the Bible. After the asking and seeking comes the knocking. After you ask and search, then knock.

Knock, and the door will open for you.

(Matt. 7:7)

To knock is to stand at God's door. To make yourself available. To climb the steps, cross the porch, stand at the doorway, and volunteer. Knocking goes beyond the realm of thinking and into the realm of acting.

To knock is to ask, What can I do? How can I obey? Where can I go?

It's one thing to know what to do. It's another to do it. But for those who do it, those who choose to obey, a special reward awaits them.

The truly happy are those who carefully study God's perfect law that makes people free, and they continue to study it. They do not forget what they heard, but they obey what God's teaching says. Those who do this will be made happy.

(James 1:25)

What a promise. Happiness comes to those who do what they read! It's the same with medicine. If you only read the label but ignore the pills, it won't help. It's the same with food. If you only read the recipe but never cook, you won't be fed. And it's the same with the Bible. If you only read the words but never obey, you'll never know the joy God has promised.

Ask. Search. Knock. Simple, isn't it? Why don't you give it a try? If you do, you'll see why you are holding the most remarkable book in history.

ROMANS

INTRODUCTION

At the moment I don't feel too smart. I just got off the wrong plane that took me to the wrong city and left me at the wrong airport. I went east instead of west and ended up in Houston instead of Denver.

It didn't look like the wrong plane, but it was. I walked through the wrong gate, dozed off on the wrong flight, and ended up in the wrong place.

Paul says we've all done the same thing. Not with airplanes and airports, but with our lives and God. He tells the Roman readers,

There is no one who always does what is right, not even one (3:10).

All have sinned and are not good enough for God's glory . . . (3:23).

We are all on the wrong plane, he says. All of us. Gentile and Jew. Every person has taken the wrong turn. And we need help.

In this profound Epistle, Paul explores all the wrong options and takes us to the only correct one. The wrong solutions are pleasure and pride (chapters 1 and 2), the correct solution is Christ Jesus (3:21–26). According to Paul, we are saved by grace (undeserved, unearned favor), through faith (complete trust) in Jesus and his work.

The letter concludes with practical instruction for a growing church, including thoughts on spiritual gifts (12:3–8); genuine love (12:9–21); good citizenship (13:1–14). The final chapters provide brilliant instruction for dealing with everything from church division to difficult brethren.

Romans is a life-changing letter for people who are willing to admit they are sinners. For those who admit they are on the wrong plane, the letter provides the correct itinerary.

Read it and take note. That flight home is one you don't want to miss.

LESSON ONE

RIGHT WITH GOD

REFLECTION

Begin your study by sharing thoughts on this question.

1. Compare your life-style before and after you became a Christian. What changes has Christ made in your life?

BIBLE READING

Read Romans 1:16–32 from the NCV or the NKJV.

NCV

[16]I am proud of the Good News, because
it is the power God uses to save everyone
who believes—to save the Jews first, and also
to save those who are not Jews. [17]The Good
News shows how God makes people right with
himself—that it begins and ends with faith.
As the Scripture says, "But those who are right
with God will live by trusting in him."

[18]God's anger is shown from heaven against
all the evil and wrong things people do. By their
own evil lives they hide the truth. [19]God shows
his anger because some knowledge of him has

NKJV

[16]For I am not ashamed of the gospel of
Christ, for it is the power of God to salvation for
everyone who believes, for the Jew first and also
for the Greek. [17]For in it the righteousness of
God is revealed from faith to faith; as it is written, "The just shall live by faith."

[18]For the wrath of God is revealed from
heaven against all ungodliness and unrighteousness of men, who suppress the truth
in unrighteousness, [19]because what may be
known of God is manifest in them, for God has
shown it to them. [20]For since the creation of the

NCV

been made clear to them. Yes, God has shown
himself to them. [20]There are things about him
that people cannot see—his eternal power and
all the things that make him God. But since the
beginning of the world those things have been
easy to understand by what God has made. So
people have no excuse for the bad things they
do. [21]They knew God, but they did not give
glory to God or thank him. Their thinking became useless. Their foolish minds were filled
with darkness. [22]They said they were wise, but
they became fools. [23]They traded the glory of
God who lives forever for the worship of idols
made to look like earthly people, birds, animals, and snakes.

[24]Because they did these things, God left
them and let them go their sinful way, wanting
only to do evil. As a result, they became full of
sexual sin, using their bodies wrongly with
each other. [25]They traded the truth of God for
a lie. They worshiped and served what had
been created instead of the God who created
those things, who should be praised forever.
Amen.

[26]Because people did those things, God left
them and let them do the shameful things they
wanted to do. Women stopped having natural
sex and started having sex with other women.
[27]In the same way, men stopped having natural sex and began wanting each other. Men did
shameful things with other men, and in their
bodies they received the punishment for those
wrongs.

[28]People did not think it was important to
have a true knowledge of God. So God left them
and allowed them to have their own worthless

NKJV

world His invisible attributes are clearly seen,
being understood by the things that are made,
even His eternal power and Godhead, so that
they are without excuse, [21]because, although
they knew God, they did not glorify Him as
God, nor were thankful, but became futile in
their thoughts, and their foolish hearts were
darkened. [22]Professing to be wise, they became
fools, [23]and changed the glory of the incorrupt-
ible God into an image made like corruptible
man—and birds and four-footed animals and
creeping things.

[24]Therefore God also gave them up to uncleanness, in the lusts of their hearts, to dis-
honor their bodies among themselves, [25]who
exchanged the truth of God for the lie, and
worshiped and served the creature rather than
the Creator, who is blessed forever. Amen.

[26]For this reason God gave them up to vile
passions. For even their women exchanged the
natural use for what is against nature. [27]Like-
wise also the men, leaving the natural use of the
woman, burned in their lust for one another,
men with men committing what is shameful,
and receiving in themselves the penalty of their
error which was due.

[28]And even as they did not like to retain God
in their knowledge, God gave them over to a
debased mind, to do those things which are not
fitting; [29]being filled with all unrighteousness,
sexual immorality, wickedness, covetousness,
maliciousness; full of envy, murder, strife, de-
ceit, evil-mindedness; they are whisperers,
[30]backbiters, haters of God, violent, proud,
boasters, inventors of evil things, disobedient
to parents, [31]undiscerning, untrustworthy,

NCV

thinking and to do things they should not do.
29They are filled with every kind of sin, evil,
selfishness, and hatred. They are full of jealousy, murder, fighting, lying, and thinking the
worst about each other. They gossip 30and say
evil things about each other. They hate God.
They are rude and conceited and brag about
themselves. They invent ways of doing evil.
They do not obey their parents. 31They are foolish, they do not keep their promises, and they
show no kindness or mercy to others. 32They
know God's law says that those who live like
this should die. But they themselves not only
continue to do these evil things, they applaud
others who do them.

NKJV

unloving, unforgiving, unmerciful; 32who,
knowing the righteous judgment of God, that
those who practice such things are deserving
of death, not only do the same but also approve
of those who practice them.

DISCOVERY

Explore the Bible reading by discussing these questions.

2. How does God reveal himself to people?

3. How have some people provoked God to anger?

4. Why is the truth of the gospel hidden from some people?

5. What happens when God lets people go their own way?

6. How can we find freedom from the bondage of sin?

INSPIRATION

Here is an uplifting thought from the *Inspirational Study Bible.*

What does it mean to be righteous? . . .

Righteousness has nothing to do with doing good works, though good works are a byproduct of being righteous. Jesus spoke of God as the only one who is truly good. The word "good" is a synonym for righteous, so it follows that to be righteous is to be like God. But how can anyone be like God, who is holy and perfect?

. . . Righteousness, meaning to be right or just, begins with believing God. It sounds so simple, but how many times do we disbelieve God? God's formulas are so simple that we ignore them because we think there must be more to it than that.

All sin is rooted in unbelief. All righteousness is rooted in belief. Believe God for all His promises and He will count it unto you as righteousness. Believe on the Lord Jesus Christ, God's ultimate standard and incarnation of righteousness, and be saved. Believe in Jesus Christ to deliver you in your day of trouble and learn what the righteousness of Christ can do in and through you.

(from *Unto the Hills*
by Billy Graham)

RESPONSE

Use these questions to share more deeply with each other.

7. How would you describe righteousness to a new believer?

____

____

____

8. Based on this passage, explain what is required to be right with God.

____

____

____

9. Have you seen the righteousness of Christ transform a person's life? Explain.

____

____

____

PRAYER

Father, forgive us for being witnesses of your majesty and yet living like you did not exist. Forgive us, Father, when we sometimes put more hope in the things of this earth than in the incredible promises of your heaven. Have mercy on our hardened hearts. Transform us into your likeness.

JOURNALING

Take a few moments to record your personal insights from this lesson.

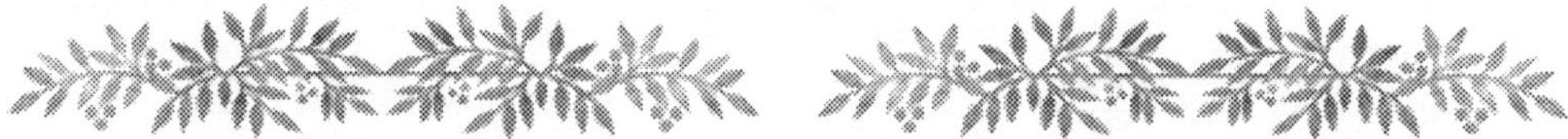

How can I thank God for saving me from a life of sin and bringing me into a right relationship with him?

ADDITIONAL QUESTIONS

10. Why is it important to establish a right relationship with God?

11. In what area of your life do your sinful desires interfere with living a righteous life?

12. How does this passage encourage you to live by faith?

For more Bible passages on righteousness, see 1 Samuel 26:23; 1 Kings 10:9; Habakkuk 2:4; Zephaniah 2:3; Malachi 4:2; Romans 3:21; 8:10; Galatians 3:11; 2 Timothy 3:16.

To complete the book of Romans during this twelve-part study, read Romans 1:1–32.

LESSON TWO

KNOWING CHRIST

REFLECTION

Begin your study by sharing thoughts on this question.

1. What steps have you taken to deepen your relationship with Christ?

____

____

____

BIBLE READING

Read Romans 2:1–16 from the NCV or the NKJV.

NCV

[1]If you think you can judge others, you are wrong. When you judge them, you are really judging yourself guilty, because you do the same things they do. [2]God judges those who do wrong things, and we know that his judging is right. [3]You judge those who do wrong, but you do wrong yourselves. Do you think you will be able to escape the judgment of God? [4]He has been very kind and patient, waiting for you to

NKJV

[1]Therefore you are inexcusable, O man, whoever you are who judge, for in whatever you judge another you condemn yourself; for you who judge practice the same things. [2]But we know that the judgment of God is according to truth against those who practice such things. [3]And do you think this, O man, you who judge those practicing such things, and doing the same, that you will escape the judgment of

NCV

change, but you think nothing of his kindness. Perhaps you do not understand that God is kind to you so you will change your hearts and lives. [5]But you are stubborn and refuse to change, so you are making your own punishment even greater on the day he shows his anger. On that day everyone will see God's right judgments. [6]God will reward or punish every person for what that person has done. [7]Some people, by always continuing to do good, live for God's glory, for honor, and for life that has no end. God will give them life forever. [8]But other people are selfish. They refuse to follow truth and, instead, follow evil. God will give them his punishment and anger. [9]He will give trouble and suffering to everyone who does evil—to the Jews first and also to those who are not Jews. [10]But he will give glory, honor, and peace to everyone who does good—to the Jews first and also to those who are not Jews. [11]For God judges all people in the same way.

[12]People who do not have the law and who are sinners will be lost, although they do not have the law. And, in the same way, those who have the law and are sinners will be judged by the law. [13]Hearing the law does not make people right with God. It is those who obey the law who will be right with him. [14](Those who are not Jews do not have the law, but when they freely do what the law commands, they are the law for themselves. This is true even though they do not have the law. [15]They show that in their hearts they know what is right and wrong, just as the law commands. And they show this by their consciences. Sometimes their thoughts tell them they did wrong, and sometimes their

NKJV

God? [4]Or do you despise the riches of His goodness, forbearance, and longsuffering, not knowing that the goodness of God leads you to repentance? [5]But in accordance with your hardness and your impenitent heart you are treasuring up for yourself wrath in the day of wrath and revelation of the righteous judgment of God, [6]who "will render to each one according to his deeds": [7]eternal life to those who by patient continuance in doing good seek for glory, honor, and immortality; [8]but to those who are self-seeking and do not obey the truth, but obey unrighteousness—indignation and wrath, [9]tribulation and anguish, on every soul of man who does evil, of the Jew first and also of the Greek; [10]but glory, honor, and peace to everyone who works what is good, to the Jew first and also to the Greek. [11]For there is no partiality with God.

[12]For as many as have sinned without law will also perish without law, and as many as have sinned in the law will be judged by the law [13](for not the hearers of the law are just in the sight of God, but the doers of the law will be justified; [14]for when Gentiles, who do not have the law, by nature do the things in the law, these, although not having the law, are a law to themselves, [15]who show the work of the law written in their hearts, their conscience also bearing witness, and between themselves their thoughts accusing or else excusing them) [16]in the day when God will judge the secrets of men by Jesus Christ, according to my gospel.

NCV

thoughts tell them they did right.) [16]All these things will happen on the day when God, through Christ Jesus, will judge people's secret thoughts. The Good News that I preach says this.

DISCOVERY

Explore the Bible reading by discussing these questions.

2. Why did Paul advise the Romans to avoid judging others?

___

___

___

3. Why do people tend to take God's kindness lightly?

___

___

___

4. What guidelines will God use to reward or punish people?

___

___

___

5. If hearing the law does not make people right with God, then what does?

____

____

____

6. How can we tell right from wrong?

____

____

____

INSPIRATION

Here is an uplifting thought from the *Inspirational Study Bible.*

I've wondered, at times, what kind of man this Judas was. What he looked like, how he acted, who his friends were. . . .

But for all the things we don't know about Judas, there is one thing we know for sure: he had no relationship with the Master. He had seen Jesus, but he did not know him. He had heard Jesus, but he did not understand him. He had religion, but no relationship.

As Satan worked his way around the table in the Upper Room, he needed a special kind of man to betray our Lord. He needed a man who had seen Jesus, but did not know him. He needed a man who knew the actions of Jesus, but had missed out on the mission of Jesus. Judas was this man. He knew the empire but had never known the Man.

We learn this timeless lesson from the betrayer. Satan's best tools of destruction are not from outside the church, they are from within the church. A church will never die from the immorality in Hollywood or the corruption in Washington. But it will die from corrosion within—from those who bear the name of Jesus but have never met him, and from those who have religion, but no relationship.

Judas bore the cloak of religion, but he never knew the heart of Christ. Let's make it our goal to know . . . deeply.

(from *On the Anvil*
by Max Lucado)

RESPONSE

Use these questions to share more deeply with each other.

7. What similarities do you see between Judas and the people Paul addressed in this letter?

8. What is the difference between being religious and being right with God?

9. Why is hypocrisy harmful to the church?

PRAYER

Father, we have all failed you in some way. We have taken wrong paths and made wrong choices. We know your law, yet we choose to ignore it. We strive to impress others with our knowledge of you when our hearts are far from you. Forgive us, Father. Guide us into a truer, deeper relationship with you.

JOURNALING

Take a few moments to record your personal insights from this lesson.

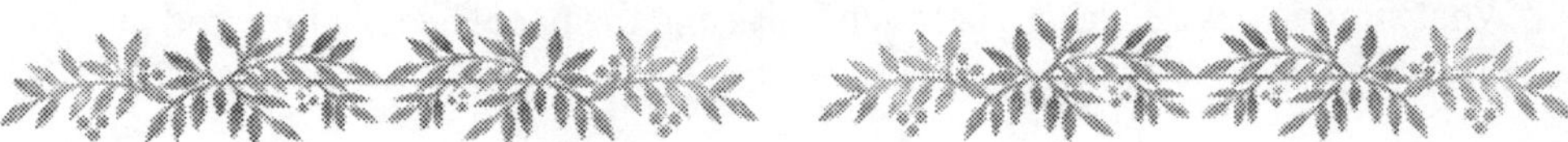

What can I do to deepen my relationship with Christ? How can I know him better?

ADDITIONAL QUESTIONS

10. What examples of spiritual corrosion do you see in the church today?

11. In what subtle ways does Satan try to corrode your relationship with Christ?

12. How can you guard against Satan's attacks?

For more Bible passages on developing a relationship with Christ, see Matthew 12:50; John 1:12; 15:5; Romans 8:15–17; 2 Corinthians 5:17; Philippians 3:8.

To complete the book of Romans during this twelve-part study, read Romans 2:1–3:8.

ADDITIONAL THOUGHTS

LESSON THREE

A PRICELESS GIFT

REFLECTION

Begin your study by sharing thoughts on this question.

1. What is the best gift you have ever received? What made it so special?

____

____

____

BIBLE READING

Read Romans 3:21–31 from the NCV or the NKJV.

NCV

21But God has a way to make people right
with him without the law, and he has now
shown us that way which the law and the
prophets told us about. 22God makes people
right with himself through their faith in Jesus
Christ. This is true for all who believe in Christ,
because all people are the same: 23All have
sinned and are not good enough for God's
glory, 24and all need to be made right with God
by his grace, which is a free gift. They need to

NKJV

21But now the righteousness of God apart
from the law is revealed, being witnessed by the
Law and the Prophets, 22even the righteousness
of God, through faith in Jesus Christ, to all and
on all who believe. For there is no difference;
23for all have sinned and fall short of the glory
of God, 24being justified freely by His grace
through the redemption that is in Christ Jesus,
25whom God set forth as a propitiation by
His blood, through faith, to demonstrate His

NCV

be made free from sin through Jesus Christ.
25God gave him as a way to forgive sin through
faith in the blood of Jesus' death. This showed
that God always does what is right and fair, as
in the past when he was patient and did not
punish people for their sins. 26And God gave
Jesus to show today that he does what is right.
God did this so he could judge rightly and so
he could make right any person who has faith
in Jesus.

27So do we have a reason to brag about ourselves? No! And why not? It is the way of faith
that stops all bragging, not the way of trying to
obey the law. 28A person is made right with God
through faith, not through obeying the law.
29Is God only the God of the Jews? Is he not also
the God of those who are not Jews? 30Of course
he is, because there is only one God. He will
make Jews right with him by their faith, and he
will also make those who are not Jews right
with him through their faith. 31So do we destroy
the law by following the way of faith? No! Faith
causes us to be what the law truly wants.

NKJV

righteousness, because in His forbearance God
had passed over the sins that were previously
committed, 26to demonstrate at the present
time His righteousness, that He might be just
and the justifier of the one who has faith in
Jesus.

27Where is boasting then? It is excluded. By
what law? Of works? No, but by the law of faith.
28Therefore we conclude that a man is justified
by faith apart from the deeds of the law. 29Or is
He the God of the Jews only? Is He not also the
God of the Gentiles? Yes, of the Gentiles also,
30since there is one God who will justify the
circumcised by faith and the uncircumcised
through faith. 31Do we then make void the law
through faith? Certainly not! On the contrary,
we establish the law.

DISCOVERY

Explore the Bible reading by discussing these questions.

2. In what way are all people alike?

3. How can people be made right with God?

4. How does God's plan demonstrate his fairness?

5. How does Paul describe salvation?

6. What should prevent believers from bragging?

INSPIRATION

Here is an uplifting thought from the *Inspirational Study Bible.*

Salvation is free! God puts no price tag on the Gift of gifts—it's free! Preachers are not salesmen for they have nothing to sell. They are bearers of Good News, the good tidings that "Christ died for our sins according to the Scriptures." Money can't buy it. Man's righteousness can't earn it. Social prestige can't help you acquire it. Morality can't purchase it. It is, as Isaiah said, "without money and without price." God is not a bargaining God. You cannot barter with Him. You must do business with Him on His own terms. He holds in His omnipotent hand the priceless, precious, eternal gift of salvation, and He bids you to take it without money and without price. The best things in life are free, are they not? The air we breathe is not sold by the cubic foot. The water which flows crystal clear from the mountain stream is free for the taking. Love is free, faith is free, hope is free.

(from *Day by Day with Billy Graham* by Joan W. Brown)

RESPONSE

Use these questions to share more deeply with each other.

7. When did you first realize that salvation is a free gift?

____

____

____

8. What helped you reach that realization?

____

____

____

9. Why do some people try to earn salvation?

PRAYER

Holy God and Father in heaven, we come to you, aware that we do not deserve to be in your presence. We thank you that you have provided a path for us through the blood of your precious Son. Your saving grace is a priceless gift. Keep us amazed and mesmerized by what you have done for us.

JOURNALING

Take a few moments to record your personal insights from this lesson.

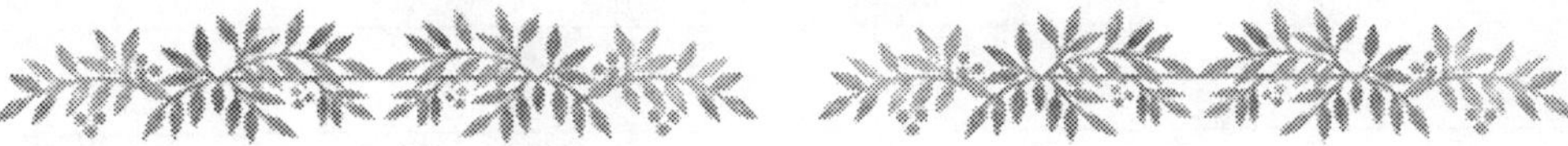

How can I tell others about God's free gift?

ADDITIONAL QUESTIONS

10. Why is it important to understand that salvation is a free gift from God?

11. Describe how your life would be different without Jesus.

12. How do we receive God's approval?

For more Bible passages on the gift of salvation, see John 3:16; Acts 4:12; Ephesians 2:8; 1 Thessalonians 5:9; 1 Timothy 1:15; Titus 2:11; Hebrews 5:7–9.

To complete the book of Romans during this twelve-part study, read Romans 3:9–31.

ADDITIONAL THOUGHTS

LESSON FOUR

THE FAITH OF ABRAHAM

REFLECTION

Begin your study by sharing thoughts on this question.

1. Think of someone who has been an example of great faith to you. What are the evidences of that person's faith?

BIBLE READING

Read Romans 4:13–25 from the NCV or the NKJV.

NCV

13Abraham and his descendants received
the promise that they would get the whole
world. He did not receive that promise through
the law, but through being right with God by
his faith. 14If people could receive what God
promised by following the law, then faith
is worthless. And God's promise to Abraham is
worthless, 15because the law can only bring
God's anger. But if there is no law, there is nothing to disobey.

NKJV

13For the promise that he would be the heir
of the world was not to Abraham or to his seed
through the law, but through the righteousness
of faith. 14For if those who are of the law are
heirs, faith is made void and the promise made
of no effect, 15because the law brings about
wrath; for where there is no law there is no
transgression.

16Therefore it is of faith that it might be according to grace, so that the promise might be

NCV

[16]So people receive God's promise by having faith. This happens so the promise can be a free gift. Then all of Abraham's children can have that promise. It is not only for those who live under the law of Moses but for anyone who lives with faith like that of Abraham, who is the father of us all. [17]As it is written in the Scriptures: "I am making you a father of many nations." This is true before God, the God Abraham believed, the God who gives life to the dead and who creates something out of nothing.

[18]There was no hope that Abraham would have children. But Abraham believed God and continued hoping, and so he became the father of many nations. As God told him, "Your descendants also will be too many to count." [19]Abraham was almost a hundred years old, much past the age for having children, and Sarah could not have children. Abraham thought about all this, but his faith in God did not become weak. [20]He never doubted that God would keep his promise, and he never stopped believing. He grew stronger in his faith and gave praise to God. [21]Abraham felt sure that God was able to do what he had promised. [22]So, "God accepted Abraham's faith, and that faith made him right with God." [23]Those words ("God accepted Abraham's faith") were written not only for Abraham [24]but also for us. God will accept us also because we believe in the One who raised Jesus our Lord from the dead. [25]Jesus was given to die for our sins, and he was raised from the dead to make us right with God.

NKJV

sure to all the seed, not only to those who are of the law, but also to those who are of the faith of Abraham, who is the father of us all [17](as it is written, "I have made you a father of many nations") in the presence of Him whom he believed—God, who gives life to the dead and calls those things which do not exist as though they did; [18]who, contrary to hope, in hope believed, so that he became the father of many nations, according to what was spoken, "So shall your descendants be." [19]And not being weak in faith, he did not consider his own body, already dead (since he was about a hundred years old), and the deadness of Sarah's womb. [20]He did not waver at the promise of God through unbelief, but was strengthened in faith, giving glory to God, [21]and being fully convinced that what He had promised He was also able to perform. [22]And therefore "it was accounted to him for righteousness."

[23]Now it was not written for his sake alone that it was imputed to him, [24]but also for us. It shall be imputed to us who believe in Him who raised up Jesus our Lord from the dead, [25]who was delivered up because of our offenses, and was raised because of our justification.

DISCOVERY

Explore the Bible reading by discussing these questions.

2. Tell how Abraham became right with God.

3. How did Abraham receive God's promise? How can others receive it?

4. What obstacles did Abraham overcome to believe God's promise?

5. What does it mean to have a strong faith?

6. What words were written for both Abraham and us?

INSPIRATION

Here is an uplifting thought from the *Inspirational Study Bible.*

Henry Drummond [writes:] "You will find, if you think for a moment, that the people who influence you are people who believe in you. In an atmosphere of suspicion men shrivel up; but in that atmosphere they expand and find encouragement and educative fellowship. It is a wonderful thing that here and there in this hard uncharitable world there should still be left a few rare souls who think no evil. This is the great unworldliness. Love sees the bright side, puts the best construction on every action. What a delightful state of mind to live in! What a stimulus and benediction even to meet with it for a day! To be trusted is to be saved. And if we try to influence or elevate others, we shall soon see that success is in proportion to their belief of our belief in them. For the respect of another is the first restoration of the self-respect a man has lost; our ideal of what he is becomes to him the hope and pattern of what he may become."

This faith moves mountains of inertia in other people. It pulverizes prejudices and impossibilities. This faith is the fruit of God's Gracious Spirit that sweetens a sour world. It replaces suspicion and distrust with friendship and hope and good cheer. It makes our friends, family, and casual acquaintances stand tall.

Faith of this caliber comes from God. If we lack it we must ask for it. He urges us to come boldly requesting good gifts from Him (Luke 11:9–13). He does bestow His Gracious Spirit on those who request His presence and are prepared to cooperate wholeheartedly with His commands (Acts 5:32). He will not withhold any good thing from those who seek His faith in sincerity. He is faithful.

(from *A Gardener Looks at the Fruits of the Spirit* by Philip Keller)

RESPONSE

Use these questions to share more deeply with each other.

7. How does Abraham's example inspire you to deeper faith?

8. How can our life of faith influence others?

9. Describe a time when someone's faith made a difference in your life.

PRAYER

Father, you accepted Abraham's faith, and you accept ours today. We do not deserve your forgiveness and mercy, yet you give it freely. Thank you for covering our guilt in the blood of your only Son. Continue to strengthen our faith in you, for your glory.

JOURNALING

Take a few moments to record your personal insights from this lesson.

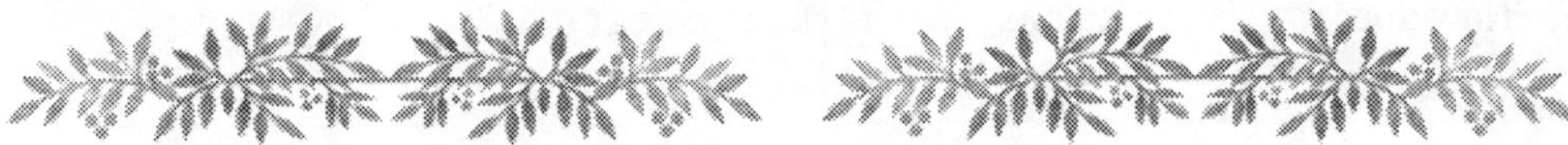

How are the people around me impacted by my faith in God?

ADDITIONAL QUESTIONS

10. What things can keep our faith from growing?

11. What can we learn from Abraham about dealing with hindrances to faith?

12. What do you usually do when you experience doubts?

For more Bible passages on faith, see Genesis 15:6; 2 Chronicles 20:20; Isaiah 7:9; Habakkuk 2:4; Matthew 9:29; Acts 15:9; Romans 5:1; 10:17.

To complete the book of Romans during this twelve-part study, read Romans 4:1–5:21.

ADDITIONAL THOUGHTS

LESSON FIVE

VICTORY OVER SIN

REFLECTION

Begin your study by sharing thoughts on this question.

1. Think of a time when you conquered a bad habit. Describe how this made you feel.

BIBLE READING

Read Romans 6:15–23 from the NCV or the NKJV.

NCV

15So what should we do? Should we sin because we are under grace and not under law?
No! 16Surely you know that when you give yourselves like slaves to obey someone, then you are
really slaves of that person. The person you
obey is your master. You can follow sin, which
brings spiritual death, or you can obey God,
which makes you right with him. 17In the past
you were slaves to sin—sin controlled you. But
thank God, you fully obeyed the things that you
were taught. 18You were made free from sin, and

NKJV

15What then? Shall we sin because we are not
under law but under grace? Certainly not! 16Do
you not know that to whom you present yourselves slaves to obey, you are that one's slaves
whom you obey, whether of sin leading to
death, or of obedience leading to righteousness? 17But God be thanked that though you
were slaves of sin, yet you obeyed from the
heart that form of doctrine to which you were
delivered. 18And having been set free from sin,
you became slaves of righteousness. 19I speak

NCV

now you are slaves to goodness. [19]I use this example because this is hard for you to understand. In the past you offered the parts of your body to be slaves to sin and evil; you lived only for evil. In the same way now you must give yourselves to be slaves of goodness. Then you will live only for God.

[20]In the past you were slaves to sin, and goodness did not control you. [21]You did evil things, and now you are ashamed of them. Those things only bring death. [22]But now you are free from sin and have become slaves of God. This brings you a life that is only for God, and this gives you life forever. [23]When people sin, they earn what sin pays—death. But God gives us a free gift—life forever in Christ Jesus our Lord.

NKJV

in human terms because of the weakness of your flesh. For just as you presented your members as slaves of uncleanness, and of lawlessness leading to more lawlessness, so now present your members as slaves of righteousness for holiness.

[20]For when you were slaves of sin, you were free in regard to righteousness. [21]What fruit did you have then in the things of which you are now ashamed? For the end of those things is death. [22]But now having been set free from sin, and having become slaves of God, you have your fruit to holiness, and the end, everlasting life. [23]For the wages of sin is death, but the gift of God is eternal life in Christ Jesus our Lord.

DISCOVERY

Explore the Bible reading by discussing these questions.

2. Why should Christians avoid sinning?

____

____

____

3. What are the consequences of sin?

4. What are the results of obeying God?

5. What example did Paul use to help the Romans understand his point?

6. What does it mean to be a slave of God?

INSPIRATION

Here is an uplifting thought from the *Inspirational Study Bible.*

Imagine being thrown in jail on suspicion of a charge, left there, virtually forgotten, while the system, ever so slowly caught up with you. You get sick. You're treated harshly. Abused. Assaulted. Would you begin to entertain that feeling of lostness and hopelessness?

Back to the question: "How shall we who died to sin still live in it?" Who would volunteer to be dumped in a jail for another series of months, having been there and suffered the consequences of such a setting? His point: Then why would emancipated slaves who have been freed from sin and shame return to live under that same domination any longer? . . .

We have been programmed to think, I know I am going to sin, to fail . . . to fall short today. Since this is true I need to be ready to find cleansing. You have not been programmed to yield yourself unto God as those who have power over sin.

How much better to begin each day thinking victory, not defeat; to awake to grace, not shame; to encounter each temptation with thoughts like, Jesus, You are my Lord and Savior. I am your child—liberated and depending on Your power. Therefore, Christ, this is Your day, to be lived for Your glory. Work through my eyes, my mouth, and through my thoughts and actions to carry out Your victory. And, Lord, do that all day long.

(from *The Grace Awakening*
by Charles Swindoll)

RESPONSE

Use these questions to share more deeply with each other.

7. Why do you think people choose to be slaves to sin?

___

___

___

8. Why do believers continue to struggle with sin?

___

___

___

9. What are the benefits of being slaves of righteousness?

PRAYER

Father, we know we can live a new life free from the bondage of sin because of the death and resurrection of your Son. You have won the victory over sin and death. Father, we ask you to be the master of our lives. Protect us from the evil one and the temptations of this world. We invite the purifying power of your Holy Spirit to cleanse our lives. May we stay blameless until the day of your return.

JOURNALING

Take a few moments to record your personal insights from this lesson.

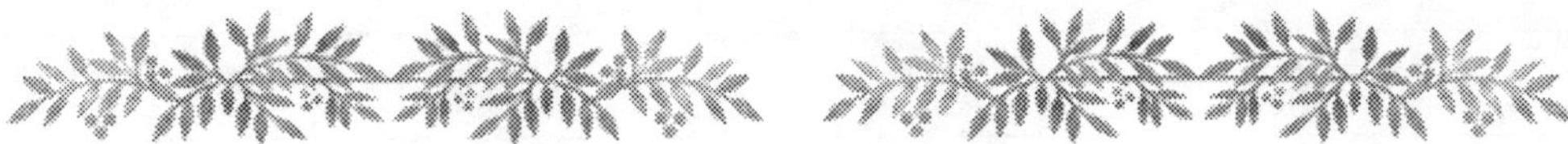

What changes do I need to make to live a more godly life?

ADDITIONAL QUESTIONS

10. Why do we let sin control areas of our lives?

11. What can a believer do to break free from sin?

12. How does this passage challenge your attitude toward sin in your life?

For more Bible passages on victory over sin, see John 1:29; 8:34–36; 1 John 1:7; 3:4–9; 5.18.

To complete the book of Romans during this twelve-part study, read Romans 6:1–23.

ADDITIONAL THOUGHTS

LESSON SIX

NOT GUILTY

REFLECTION

Begin your study by sharing thoughts on this question.

1. How does it feel to be "let off the hook" after doing something wrong?

____

____

____

BIBLE READING

Read Romans 8:1–17 from the NCV or the NKJV.

NCV

[1]So now, those who are in Christ Jesus are
not judged guilty. [2]Through Christ Jesus the law
of the Spirit that brings life made me free from
the law that brings sin and death. [3]The law was
without power, because the law was made weak
by our sinful selves. But God did what the law
could not do. He sent his own Son to earth with
the same human life that others use for sin. By
sending his Son to be an offering to pay for sin,
God used a human life to destroy sin. [4]He did
this so that we could be the kind of people the

NKJV

[1]There is therefore now no condemnation to
those who are in Christ Jesus, who do not walk
according to the flesh, but according to the
Spirit. [2]For the law of the Spirit of life in Christ
Jesus has made me free from the law of sin and
death. [3]For what the law could not do in that it
was weak through the flesh, God did by sending His own Son in the likeness of sinful flesh,
on account of sin: He condemned sin in the
flesh, [4]that the righteous requirement of the
law might be fulfilled in us who do not walk

NCV

law correctly wants us to be. Now we do not live following our sinful selves, but we live following the Spirit.

5Those who live following their sinful selves think only about things that their sinful selves want. But those who live following the Spirit are thinking about the things the Spirit wants them to do. 6If people's thinking is controlled by the sinful self, there is death. But if their thinking is controlled by the Spirit, there is life and peace. 7When people's thinking is controlled by the sinful self, they are against God, because they refuse to obey God's law and really are not even able to obey God's law. 8Those people who are ruled by their sinful selves cannot please God.

9But you are not ruled by your sinful selves. You are ruled by the Spirit, if that Spirit of God really lives in you. But the person who does not have the Spirit of Christ does not belong to Christ. 10Your body will always be dead because of sin. But if Christ is in you, then the Spirit gives you life, because Christ made you right with God. 11God raised Jesus from the dead, and if God's Spirit is living in you, he will also give life to your bodies that die. God is the One who raised Christ from the dead, and he will give life through his Spirit that lives in you.

12So, my brothers and sisters, we must not be ruled by our sinful selves or live the way our sinful selves want. 13If you use your lives to do the wrong things your sinful selves want, you will die spiritually. But if you use the Spirit's help to stop doing the wrong things you do with your body, you will have true life.

14The true children of God are those who let

NKJV

according to the flesh but according to the Spirit. 5For those who live according to the flesh set their minds on the things of the flesh, but those who live according to the Spirit, the things of the Spirit. 6For to be carnally minded is death, but to be spiritually minded is life and peace. 7Because the carnal mind is enmity against God; for it is not subject to the law of God, nor indeed can be. 8So then, those who are in the flesh cannot please God.

9But you are not in the flesh but in the Spirit, if indeed the Spirit of God dwells in you. Now if anyone does not have the Spirit of Christ, he is not His. 10And if Christ is in you, the body is dead because of sin, but the Spirit is life because of righteousness. 11But if the Spirit of Him who raised Jesus from the dead dwells in you, He who raised Christ from the dead will also give life to your mortal bodies through His Spirit who dwells in you.

12Therefore, brethren, we are debtors—not to the flesh, to live according to the flesh. 13For if you live according to the flesh you will die; but if by the Spirit you put to death the deeds of the body, you will live. 14For as many as are led by the Spirit of God, these are sons of God. 15For you did not receive the spirit of bondage again to fear, but you received the Spirit of adoption by whom we cry out, "Abba, Father." 16The Spirit Himself bears witness with our spirit that we are children of God, 17and if children, then heirs—heirs of God and joint heirs with Christ, if indeed we suffer with Him, that we may also be glorified together.

NCV

God's Spirit lead them. 15The Spirit we received
does not make us slaves again to fear; it makes
us children of God. With that Spirit we cry out,
"Father." 16And the Spirit himself joins with our
spirits to say we are God's children. 17If we are
God's children, we will receive blessings from
God together with Christ. But we must suffer
as Christ suffered so that we will have glory as
Christ has glory.

DISCOVERY

Explore the Bible reading by discussing these questions.

2. Explain how the law could not provide salvation.

____

____

____

3. Who is unable to please God? Why?

____

____

____

4. In what ways does the Spirit of God transform people?

____

____

____

5. How can a person attain true life?

____

____

____

6. Explain what it means to live by the Spirit.

____

____

____

INSPIRATION

Here is an uplifting thought from the *Inspirational Study Bible.*

The Bible says the judgment for sin that I deserved is already passed. Christ took my judgment on the cross. Every demand of the law has been met. The law was completely satisfied in the offering that Christ made of Himself for sins. . . .

I deserved judgment and hell, but Christ took that judgment and hell for me. . . .

We shall never understand the extent of God's love in Christ at the cross until we understand that we shall never have to stand before the judgment of God for our sins. Christ took our sins. He finished the work of redemption. I am not saved through any works or merit of my own. I have preached to thousands of people on every continent, but I shall not go to heaven because I am a preacher. I am going to heaven entirely on the merit of the work of Christ. I shall never stand at God's judgment bar. That is all past.

(from *Unto the Hills*
by Billy Graham)

RESPONSE

Use these questions to share more deeply with each other.

7. How does the truth of this passage motivate you to live your life?

8. How has your life changed since you began your new life in Christ?

9. How should believers deal with feelings of condemnation and guilt?

PRAYER

Father, we want to come to you, but sometimes we are too ashamed of who we are and what we have done. We're afraid that we have done something unforgivable, afraid that you will reject us. But Father, your Word teaches us that you sacrificed your Son as the atonement for our sin. There is no sin too deep for your hand of forgiveness to reach. Thank you, Father, for the assurance that we are forgiven and acceptable in your sight.

JOURNALING

Take a few moments to record your personal insights from this lesson.

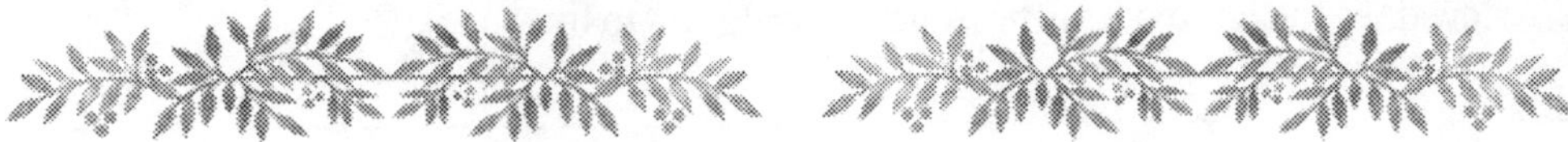

How do I feel about being judged "not guilty" by God?

ADDITIONAL QUESTIONS

10. What new perspective does this study give you about Christ's sacrifice?

____

____

____

11. What evidence of the Holy Spirit's control can people see in your life?

____

____

____

12. In what areas do you need to depend more on the Holy Spirit and less on your own desires?

____

____

____

For more Bible passages on Christ's sacrifice for sin, see John 1:29; Romans 3:25; 2 Corinthians 5:21; Hebrews 9:26–28; 10:19–22; 1 Peter 2:24; 1 John 2:2; 4:10.

To complete the book of Romans during this twelve-part study, read Romans 7:1–8:39.

ADDITIONAL THOUGHTS

LESSON SEVEN

GOD'S PERFECT PLAN

REFLECTION

Begin your study by sharing thoughts on this question.

1. When did you first hear the gospel message? What was your initial response?

____

____

____

BIBLE READING

Read Romans 10:1–15 from the NCV or the NKJV.

NCV

1Brothers and sisters, the thing I want most is for all the Jews to be saved. That is my prayer to God. 2I can say this about them: They really try to follow God, but they do not know the right way. 3Because they did not know the way that God makes people right with him, they tried to make themselves right in their own way. So they did not accept God's way of making people right. 4Christ ended the law so that everyone who believes in him may be right with God.

5Moses writes about being made right by

NKJV

1Brethren, my heart's desire and prayer to God for Israel is that they may be saved. 2For I bear them witness that they have a zeal for God, but not according to knowledge. 3For they being ignorant of God's righteousness, and seeking to establish their own righteousness, have not submitted to the righteousness of God. 4For Christ is the end of the law for righteousness to everyone who believes.

5For Moses writes about the righteousness which is of the law, "The man who does those things shall live by them." 6But the

NCV

following the law. He says, "A person who obeys
these things will live because of them." 6But this
is what the Scripture says about being made
right through faith: "Don't say to yourself,
'Who will go up into heaven?' " (That means,
"Who will go up to heaven and bring Christ
down to earth?") 7"And do not say, 'Who will go
down into the world below?'" (That means,
"Who will go down and bring Christ up from
the dead?") 8This is what the Scripture says:
"The word is near you; it is in your mouth and
in your heart." That is the teaching of faith that
we are telling. 9If you use your mouth to say,
"Jesus is Lord," and if you believe in your heart
that God raised Jesus from the dead, you will
be saved. 10We believe with our hearts, and
so we are made right with God. And we use
our mouths to say that we believe, and so we
are saved. 11As the Scripture says, "Anyone
who trusts in him will never be disappointed."
12That Scripture says "anyone" because there is
no difference between those who are Jews and
those who are not. The same Lord is the Lord
of all and gives many blessings to all who trust
in him, 13as the Scripture says, "Anyone who
calls on the Lord will be saved."

14But before people can ask the Lord for help,
they must believe in him; and before they can
believe in him, they must hear about him; and
for them to hear about the Lord, someone must
tell them; 15and before someone can go and tell
them, that person must be sent. It is written,
"How beautiful is the person who comes to
bring good news."

NKJV

righteousness of faith speaks in this way, "Do
not say in your heart, 'Who will ascend into
heaven?' " (that is, to bring Christ down from
above) 7or, " 'Who will descend into the abyss?'
" (that is, to bring Christ up from the dead).
8But what does it say? "The word is near you,
in your mouth and in your heart" (that is, the
word of faith which we preach): 9that if you
confess with your mouth the Lord Jesus and
believe in your heart that God has raised Him
from the dead, you will be saved. 10For with the
heart one believes unto righteousness, and
with the mouth confession is made unto
salvation. 11For the Scripture says, "Whoever
believes on Him will not be put to shame." 12For
there is no distinction between Jew and Greek,
for the same Lord over all is rich to all who call
upon Him. 13For "whoever calls on the name of
the LORD shall be saved."

14How then shall they call on Him in whom
they have not believed? And how shall they
believe in Him of whom they have not heard?
And how shall they hear without a preacher?
15And how shall they preach unless they are
sent? As it is written:

"How beautiful are the feet of
those who preach the gospel of peace,
Who bring glad tidings of good things!"

DISCOVERY

Explore the Bible reading by discussing these questions.

2. What is wrong with trying to be saved your own way?

3. What part do our thoughts and our words have in our response to salvation?

4. What promise is given to people who believe and confess that Jesus is Lord?

5. How does God's righteousness motivate us to godly behavior?

6. What does this passage teach about the way the good news is spread, understood, and accepted?

____

____

____

INSPIRATION

Here is an uplifting thought from the *Inspirational Study Bible.*

We have already seen that the Bible teaches that God was a God of love. He wanted to do something for man. He wanted to save man. He wanted to free man from the curse of sin. How could He do it? God was a just God. He was righteous, and holy. He had warned man from the beginning that if he obeyed the Devil and disobeyed God, he would die physically and spiritually. . . .

All through the Old Testament, God gave man the promise of salvation if by faith he would believe in the coming Redeemer. Therefore God began to teach His people that man could only be saved by substitution. Someone else would have to pay the bill for man's redemption. . . .

Thanks be to God—that is exactly what happened! Looking down over the battlements of heaven He saw this planet swinging in space—doomed, damned, crushed, and bound for hell. He saw you and me struggling beneath our load of sin and bound in the chains and ropes of sin. He made His decision in the council halls of God. The angelic hosts bowed in humility and awe as heaven's Prince of Princes and Lord of Lords, who could speak worlds into space, got into His jeweled chariot, went through pearly gates, across the steep of the skies, and on a black Judean night, while the stars sang together and the escorting angels chanted praises, stepped out of the chariot, threw off His robes, and became man!

(from *Peace with God*
by Billy Graham)

RESPONSE

Use these questions to share more deeply with each other.

7. What aspects of God's character are shown through his plan of salvation?

8. How are you encouraged by God's plan to save the world?

9. Why is it difficult for us to follow Jesus?

PRAYER

Father, help us understand that your plan is based on love—not on our performance. Help us to be captivated by your love. To be overwhelmed by your grace. To come home to you in that beautiful path that you've already carved out for us.

JOURNALING

Take a few moments to record your personal insights from this lesson.

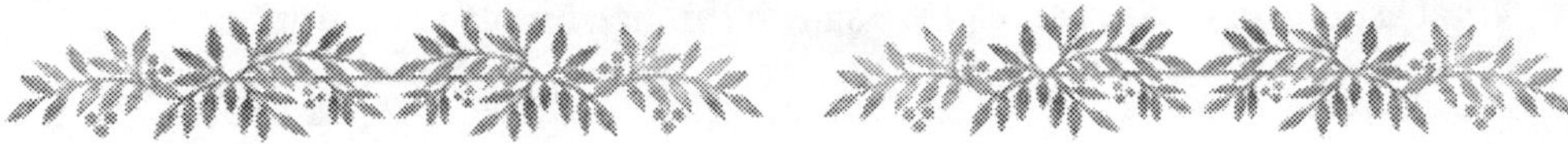

How can my life reflect the righteousness of God?

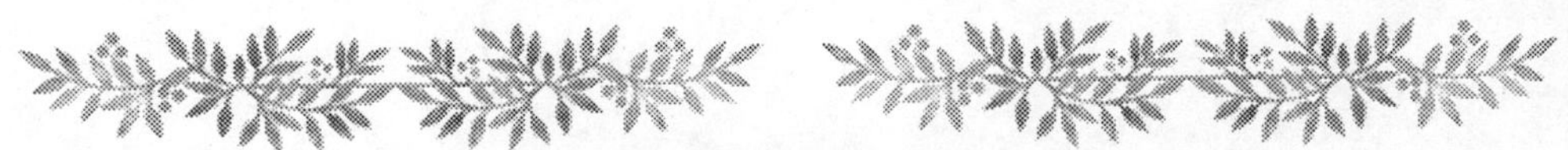

ADDITIONAL QUESTIONS

10. What can we learn from Israel's response to God's plan of salvation?

11. How can you guard against trying to earn God's approval and acceptance?

12. Why is it important to tell others about your faith in Jesus Christ?

For more Bible passages on God's plan of salvation, see John 3:16; 4:22; Acts 4:12; 28:28; 2 Corinthians 7:10; 1 Thessalonians 5:9; Revelation 7:10.

To complete the book of Romans during this twelve-part study, read Romans 9:1–10:21.

ADDITIONAL THOUGHTS

LESSON EIGHT

CALLED BY GOD

REFLECTION

Begin your study by sharing thoughts on this question.

1. Think of a time when you were given a special honor or privilege. How did that recognition make you feel?

BIBLE READING

Read Romans 11:1–15 from the NCV or the NKJV.

NCV

[1]So I ask: Did God throw out his people? No! I myself am an Israelite from the family of Abraham, from the tribe of Benjamin. [2]God chose the Israelites to be his people before they were born, and he has not thrown his people out. Surely you know what the Scripture says about Elijah, how he prayed to God against the people of Israel. [3]"Lord," he said, "they have killed your prophets, and they have destroyed your altars. I am the only prophet left, and now they are trying to kill me, too." [4]But what

NKJV

[1]I say then, has God cast away His people? Certainly not! For I also am an Israelite, of the seed of Abraham, of the tribe of Benjamin. [2]God has not cast away His people whom He foreknew. Or do you not know what the Scripture says of Elijah, how he pleads with God against Israel, saying, [3]"LORD, they have killed Your prophets and torn down Your altars, and I alone am left, and they seek my life"? [4]But what does the divine response say to him? "I have reserved for Myself seven thousand men

NCV

answer did God give Elijah? He said, "But I have
left seven thousand people in Israel who have
never bowed down before Baal." 5It is the same
now. There are a few people that God has chosen by his grace. 6And if he chose them by
grace, it is not for the things they have done.
If they could be made God's people by what
they did, God's gift of grace would not really
be a gift.

7So this is what has happened: Although the
Israelites tried to be right with God, they did
not succeed, but the ones God chose did become right with him. The others were made
stubborn and refused to listen to God. 8As it is
written in the Scriptures:

"God gave the people a dull mind so
they could not understand."

"He closed their eyes so they could not see
and their ears so they could not hear.
This continues until today."

9And David says:

"Let their own feasts trap them and
cause their ruin;
let their feasts cause them to stumble
and be paid back.
10Let their eyes be closed so they cannot see
and their backs be forever weak from
troubles."

11So I ask: When the Jews fell, did that fall
destroy them? No! But their mistake brought
salvation to those who are not Jews, in order to
make the Jews jealous. 12The Jews' mistake
brought rich blessings for the world, and the
Jews' loss brought rich blessings for the non-
Jewish people. So surely the world will receive

NKJV

who have not bowed the knee to Baal." 5Even so
then, at this present time there is a remnant
according to the election of grace. 6And if by
grace, then it is no longer of works; otherwise
grace is no longer grace. But if it is of works,
it is no longer grace; otherwise work is no
longer work.

7What then? Israel has not obtained what it
seeks; but the elect have obtained it, and the
rest were blinded. 8Just as it is written:

"God has given them a spirit of stupor,
Eyes that they should not see
And ears that they should not hear,
To this very day."

9And David says:

"Let their table become a snare and a trap,
A stumbling block and a recompense to
them.
10 Let their eyes be darkened, so that they do
not see,
And bow down their back always."

11I say then, have they stumbled that they
should fall? Certainly not! But through their
fall, to provoke them to jealousy, salvation has
come to the Gentiles. 12Now if their fall is riches
for the world, and their failure riches for the
Gentiles, how much more their fullness!

13For I speak to you Gentiles; inasmuch as I
am an apostle to the Gentiles, I magnify my
ministry, 14if by any means I may provoke to
jealousy those who are my flesh and save some
of them. 15For if their being cast away is the

NCV

much richer blessings when enough Jews become the kind of people God wants.

13Now I am speaking to you who are not Jews. I am an apostle to those who are not Jews, and since I have that work, I will make the most
of it. 14I hope I can make my own people jealous and, in that way, help some of them to be
saved. 15When God turned away from the Jews, he became friends with other people in the world. So when God accepts the Jews, surely that will bring them life after death.

NKJV

reconciling of the world, what will their acceptance be but life from the dead?

DISCOVERY

Explore the Bible reading by discussing these questions.

2. Why did people think that God must have rejected the Israelites?

3. What does God's answer to Elijah show us?

4. How do people try to earn God's grace?

5. Why are some people open to the Good News and others are closed?

6. Why can we be confident that God's grace is for all who will receive it?

INSPIRATION

Here is an uplifting thought from the *Inspirational Study Bible.*

The fact that God has chosen some to be saved does not mean that He has chosen the rest to be lost. The world is already lost and dead in sins. If left to ourselves, all of us would be condemned eternally. The question is, Does God have a right to stoop down, take a handful of already doomed clay, and fashion a vessel of beauty out of it? Of course He does. C. R. Erdman put it in right perspective when he said, "God's sovereignty is never exercised in condemning men who ought to be saved, but rather it has resulted in the salvation of men who ought to be lost."

The only way people can know if they are among the elect is by trusting Jesus Christ as Lord and Savior (1Thessalonians. 1:4–7). God holds people responsible to accept the Savior by an act of the will. In reproving those Jews who did not believe, Jesus placed the blame on their will. He did *not* say, "You cannot come to Me because you are not chosen." Rather, He *did* say, "You *are not willing* to come to Me that you may have life" (John 5:40, emphasis added).

The real question of a believer is not, Does the sovereign God have the right to choose people to be saved? Rather, it is, Why did He choose *me*? This should make a person a worshiper for all eternity.

(from *Alone in Majesty*
by William MacDonald)

RESPONSE

Use these questions to share more deeply with each other.

7. What hope does God offer to all people?

___

___

___

8. What can you learn from this passage about God's sovereignty and our responsibility?

____

____

____

9. What things does this passage make you feel grateful for?

____

____

____

PRAYER

O Sovereign God, you are beyond our understanding. Your ways are perfect; your unlimited mercy astounds us. Thank you for calling us to yourself and claiming us for your own. Teach us to trust you more, to love you deeply, and to turn to you in humility every day.

JOURNALING

Take a few moments to record your personal insights from this lesson.

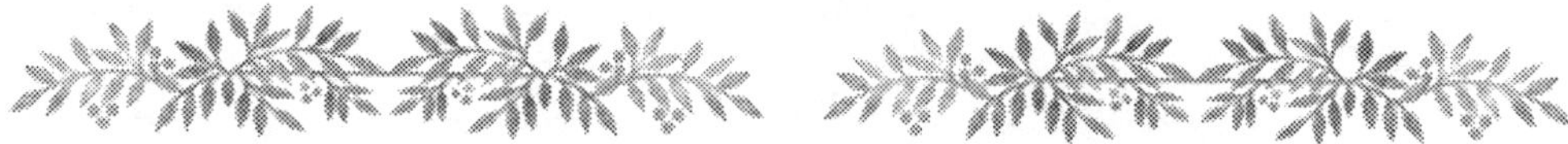

How have I responded to God's call on my life?

ADDITIONAL QUESTIONS

10. How are some people misled about the true way of salvation?

11. In what different things do people put their hope for salvation?

12. Why is it important that we not take our salvation for granted?

For more Bible passages on the way God chooses to save, see Deuteronomy 9:4, 5; Romans 2:4; 8:28, 29; Ephesians 1:4–6, 11; 2:8, 9; 1 Timothy 2:3, 4; Titus 3:4, 5.

To complete the book of Romans during this twelve-part study, read Romans 11:1–36.

LESSON NINE

THE BIG PICTURE

REFLECTION

Begin your study by sharing thoughts on this question.

1. Describe a time when someone you know was joyful during a trial. How did this affect you?

BIBLE READING

Read Romans 12:1–13 from the NCV or the NKJV.

NCV

1So brothers and sisters, since God has
shown us great mercy, I beg you to offer your
lives as a living sacrifice to him. Your offering
must be only for God and pleasing to him,
which is the spiritual way for you to worship.
2Do not change yourselves to be like the people
of this world, but be changed within by a new
way of thinking. Then you will be able to decide what God wants for you; you will know
what is good and pleasing to him and what is

NKJV

1I beseech you therefore, brethren, by the
mercies of God, that you present your bodies a
living sacrifice, holy, acceptable to God, which
is your reasonable service. 2And do not be con-
formed to this world, but be transformed by the
renewing of your mind, that you may prove
what is that good and acceptable and perfect
will of God.

3For I say, through the grace given to me, to
everyone who is among you, not to think of

NCV

perfect. [3]Because God has given me a special gift, I have something to say to everyone among you. Do not think you are better than you are. You must decide what you really are by the amount of faith God has given you. [4]Each one of us has a body with many parts, and these parts all have different uses. [5]In the same way, we are many, but in Christ we are all one body. Each one is a part of that body, and each part belongs to all the other parts. [6]We all have different gifts, each of which came because of the grace God gave us. The person who has the gift of prophecy should use that gift in agreement with the faith. [7]Anyone who has the gift of serving should serve. Anyone who has the gift of teaching should teach. [8]Whoever has the gift of encouraging others should encourage. Whoever has the gift of giving to others should give freely. Anyone who has the gift of being a leader should try hard when he leads. Whoever has the gift of showing mercy to others should do so with joy.

[9]Your love must be real. Hate what is evil, and hold on to what is good. [10]Love each other like brothers and sisters. Give each other more honor than you want for yourselves. [11]Do not be lazy but work hard, serving the Lord with all your heart. [12]Be joyful because you have hope. Be patient when trouble comes, and pray at all times. [13]Share with God's people who need help. Bring strangers in need into your homes.

NKJV

himself more highly than he ought to think, but to think soberly, as God has dealt to each one a measure of faith. [4]For as we have many members in one body, but all the members do not have the same function, [5]so we, being many, are one body in Christ, and individually members of one another. [6]Having then gifts differing according to the grace that is given to us, let us use them: if prophecy, let us prophesy in proportion to our faith; [7]or ministry, let us use it in our ministering; he who teaches, in teaching; [8]he who exhorts, in exhortation; he who gives, with liberality; he who leads, with diligence; he who shows mercy, with cheerfulness.

[9]Let love be without hypocrisy. Abhor what is evil. Cling to what is good. [10]Be kindly affectionate to one another with brotherly love, in honor giving preference to one another; [11]not lagging in diligence, fervent in spirit, serving the Lord; [12]rejoicing in hope, patient in tribulation, continuing steadfastly in prayer; [13]distributing to the needs of the saints, given to hospitality.

DISCOVERY

Explore the Bible reading by discussing these questions.

2. What does it mean to be a living sacrifice?

3. What does Paul mean when he tells us to be changed within by a new way of thinking?

4. What hinders Christians from thinking and acting like parts of one body?

5. What advice does this passage offer about getting along with each other?

6. How should we react during times of trouble?

INSPIRATION

Here is an uplifting thought from the *Inspirational Study Bible.*

Would you buy a house if you were only allowed to see one of its rooms? Would you purchase a car if you were permitted to see only its tires and a taillight? Would you pass judgment on a book after reading only one paragraph?

Nor would I.

Good judgment requires a broad picture. Not only is that true in purchasing houses, cars, and books, it's true in evaluating life. One failure doesn't make a person a failure; one achievement doesn't make a person a success.

"The end of the matter is better than its beginning," penned the sage.

"Be . . . patient in affliction," echoed the apostle Paul. . . .

We only have a fragment. Life's mishaps and horrors are only a page out of a grand book. We must be slow about drawing conclusions. We must reserve judgment on life's storms until we know the whole story. . . .

"Do not worry about tomorrow, for tomorrow will worry about itself."

He should know. He is the Author of our story. And he has already written the final chapter.

(from *In the Eye of the Storm*
by Max Lucado)

RESPONSE

Use these questions to share more deeply with each other.

7. Why is it difficult to wait for God to act on our behalf?

8. Is it difficult for you to be patient when you face trouble? Why or why not?

9. List some areas of your life where you need to be more patient.

PRAYER

God of peace, teach us what it means to be peacemakers. Help us to cultivate peace between others and you—in our neighborhoods, offices, and schoolrooms. Teach us to rely on you to defend us instead of constantly sticking up for ourselves. Teach us the art of building bridges and not walls. May we be slow to judge and quick to forgive.

JOURNALING

Take a few moments to record your personal insights from this lesson.

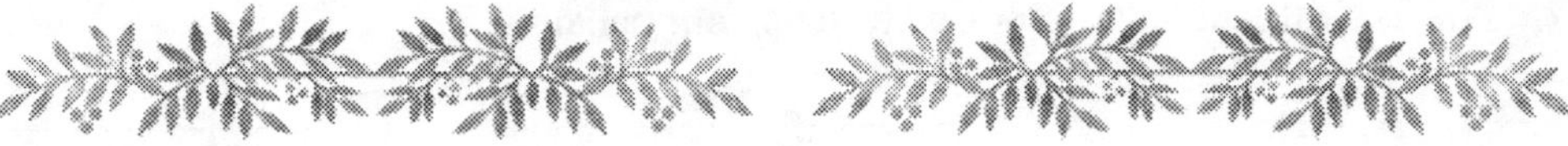

Tell God about the troubles you face.

ADDITIONAL QUESTIONS

10. How is it possible for troubles to be a blessing?

11. What spiritual gifts do you think God has given you?

12. What does it mean to serve God with all your heart?

For more Bible passages on patience in affliction, see Job 36:15; Psalm 22:24; 107:41; Isaiah 49:13; Romans 5:3–5; 2 Corinthians 1:6; Colossians 1:11; James 5:10; 1 Peter 4:13; Revelation 1:9.

To complete the book of Romans during this twelve-part study, read Romans 12:1–21.

ADDITIONAL THOUGHTS

LESSON TEN

TRUE LOVE

REFLECTION

Begin your study by sharing thoughts on this question.

1. Think of a time when a friend showed love for you in a special way. How did that make you feel? How did you respond?

___

___

___

BIBLE READING

Read Romans 13:8–14 from the NCV or the NKJV.

NCV

[8]Do not owe people anything, except always owe love to each other, because the person who loves others has obeyed all the law. [9]The law says, "You must not be guilty of adultery. You must not murder anyone. You must not steal. You must not want to take your neighbor's things." All these commands and all others are really only one rule: "Love your neighbor as you love yourself." [10]Love never hurts a neighbor, so loving is obeying all the law.

[11]Do this because we live in an important

NKJV

[8]Owe no one anything except to love one another, for he who loves another has fulfilled the law. [9]For the commandments, "You shall not commit adultery," "You shall not murder," "You shall not steal," "You shall not bear false witness," "You shall not covet," and if there is any other commandment, are all summed up in this saying, namely, "You shall love your neighbor as yourself." [10]Love does no harm to a neighbor; therefore love is the fulfillment of the law.

NCV

time. It is now time for you to wake up from
your sleep, because our salvation is nearer now
than when we first believed. 12The "night" is
almost finished, and the "day" is almost here.
So we should stop doing things that belong to
darkness and take up the weapons used for
fighting in the light. 13Let us live in a right way,
like people who belong to the day. We should
not have wild parties or get drunk. There
should be no sexual sins of any kind, no fighting or jealousy. 14But clothe yourselves with the
Lord Jesus Christ and forget about satisfying
your sinful self.

NKJV

11And do this, knowing the time, that now
it is high time to awake out of sleep; for now our
salvation is nearer than when we first believed.
12The night is far spent, the day is at hand.
Therefore let us cast off the works of darkness,
and let us put on the armor of light. 13Let us
walk properly, as in the day, not in revelry and
drunkenness, not in lewdness and lust, not in
strife and envy. 14But put on the Lord Jesus
Christ, and make no provision for the flesh, to
fulfill its lusts.

DISCOVERY

Explore the Bible reading by discussing these questions.

2. What is the one debt we owe to each other?

____

____

____

3. What one rule sums up the whole law?

____

____

____

4. Write in your own words how this passage describes true love.

5. What does Paul mean when he describes believers as "people who belong to the day"?

6. How can we "put on" or "clothe" ourselves with the Lord Jesus?

INSPIRATION

Here is an uplifting thought from the *Inspirational Study Bible.*

We aren't always sure ourselves what we mean when we use the term *love*. That word has become one of the most widely misused words in our language. We use the word love to describe the basest as well as the most exalted of human relationships. We say we "love" to travel, we "love" to eat chocolate cake, we "love" our new car, or the pattern in the wallpaper in our home. Why, we even say we "love" our neighbors—but most of us don't do much more than just say it and let it go at that! No wonder we don't have a very clear idea of what the Bible means when it says: "God is Love."

Don't make the mistake of thinking that because God is Love that everything is going to be sweet, beautiful, and happy and that no one will be punished for his sins. God's holiness demands that all sin be punished, but God's love provides the plan and way of redemption for sinful man. God's love is the cross of Jesus, by which man can have forgiveness and cleansing. It was the love of God that sent Jesus Christ to the cross!

Never question God's great love, for it is as unchangeable a part of God as His holiness. No matter how terrible your sins, God loves you. Were it not for the love of God, none of us would ever have a chance in the future life. But God is Love and his love for us is everlasting!

(from *Peace with God*
by Billy Graham)

RESPONSE

Use these questions to share more deeply with each other.

7. What are some of the misconceptions people have about love?

____

____

____

8. How is God's view of love different from the world's view?

9. Why is it important that we love others?

PRAYER

God, help us to show your love to those around us. Open our eyes to people who are in desperate need of a loving touch. Let our lives be testimonies of your love for us, so that when people see us, they will feel your love for them.

JOURNALING

Take a few moments to record your personal insights from this lesson.

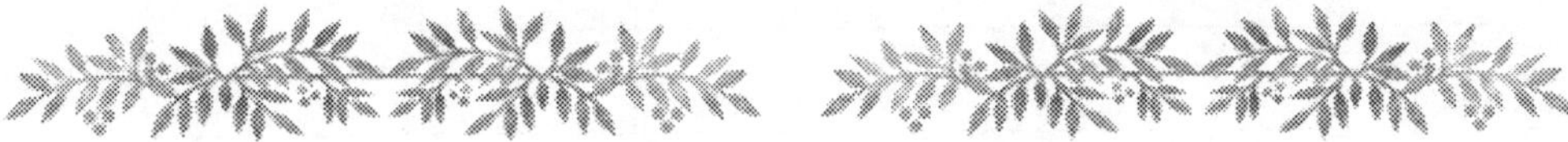

What motivates me to love others? What prevents me from loving others?

ADDITIONAL QUESTIONS

10. How do you usually respond to the "unlovable people" in our society?

11. In what ways do you demonstrate your love for your friends?

12. Think of a person who needs to feel God's love. How can you demonstrate God's love to that person?

For more Bible passages on loving others, see John 15:9–13; 1 Corinthians 13; Galatians 5:13, 14; Ephesians 5:1, 2; Colossians 3:12–14; 1 Peter 1:22; 1 John 3:11–23; 4:7, 8.

To complete the book of Romans during this twelve-part study, read Romans 13:1–14.

ADDITIONAL THOUGHTS

LESSON ELEVEN

ACCEPTING ONE ANOTHER

REFLECTION

Begin your study by sharing thoughts on this question.

1. Describe a particular time when you sensed a spirit of unity among Christians.

____

____

____

BIBLE READING

Read Romans 14:13–23 from the NCV or the NKJV.

NCV

13For that reason we should stop judging each other. We must make up our minds not to do anything that will make another Christian sin.
14I am in the Lord Jesus, and I know that there is no food that is wrong to eat. But if a person believes something is wrong, that thing is wrong for him.
15If you hurt your brother's or sister's faith because of something you eat, you are not really following the way of love. Do not destroy someone's faith by eating food he thinks is wrong, because Christ died for him.

NKJV

13Therefore let us not judge one another anymore, but rather resolve this, not to put a stumbling block or a cause to fall in our brother's way.

14I know and am convinced by the Lord Jesus that there is nothing unclean of itself; but to him who considers anything to be unclean, to him it is unclean.
15Yet if your brother is grieved because of your food, you are no longer walking in love. Do not destroy with your food the one for whom Christ died.
16Therefore do

NCV

16Do not allow what you think is good to become what others say is evil. 17In the kingdom
of God, eating and drinking are not important.
The important things are living right with God,
peace, and joy in the Holy Spirit. 18Anyone who
serves Christ by living this way is pleasing God
and will be accepted by other people.

19So let us try to do what makes peace and
helps one another. 20Do not let the eating of
food destroy the work of God. All foods are all
right to eat, but it is wrong to eat food that
causes someone else to sin. 21It is better not to
eat meat or drink wine or do anything that will
cause your brother or sister to sin.

22Your beliefs about these things should be
kept secret between you and God. People are
happy if they can do what they think is right
without feeling guilty. 23But those who eat
something without being sure it is right are
wrong because they did not believe it was right.
Anything that is done without believing it is
right is a sin.

NKJV

not let your good be spoken of as evil; 17for the
kingdom of God is not eating and drinking,
but righteousness and peace and joy in the
Holy Spirit. 18For he who serves Christ in these
things is acceptable to God and approved
by men.

19Therefore let us pursue the things which
make for peace and the things by which one
may edify another. 20Do not destroy the work
of God for the sake of food. All things indeed
are pure, but it is evil for the man who eats with
offense. 21It is good neither to eat meat nor
drink wine nor do anything by which your
brother stumbles or is offended or is made
weak. 22Do you have faith? Have it to yourself
before God. Happy is he who does not condemn
himself in what he approves. 23But he who
doubts is condemned if he eats, because he
does not eat from faith; for whatever is not
from faith is sin.

DISCOVERY

Explore the Bible reading by discussing these questions.

2. What issues caused division among the believers in Rome?

____

____

____

3. How did Paul counsel the Roman believers to deal with these issues?

4. What is the key point that Paul made in this passage?

5. When should Christians defer to a fellow believer's beliefs?

6. Explain why it is more important to maintain unity than to maintain our personal rights.

INSPIRATION

Here is an uplifting thought from the *Inspirational Study Bible.*

Accepting others is basic to letting them be. The problem [in Paul's day] was not a meat problem, it was a love problem, an acceptance problem. It still is. How often we restrict our love by making it conditional: "If you will (or won't), then I will accept you." Paul starts there: "Accept one another!" . . . Those who didn't eat [meat] (called here "weak in the faith") were exhorted to accept and not judge those who ate. And those who ate were exhorted to accept and not regard with contempt those who did not eat. The secret lies in accepting one another. All of this is fairly easy to read so long as I stay on the issue of eating meat. That one is safe because it isn't a current taboo. It's easy to accept those folks today because they don't exist!

How about those in our life who may disagree with us on issues that are taboos in evangelical Christian circles today? . . . Going to movies . . . Playing cards . . . Not having a "quiet time" every morning . . . Going to a restaurant that sells liquor . . . Listening to certain music . . . Dancing . . . Drinking coffee . . .

There are a dozen other things I could list, some of which would make you smile. But believe me, in various areas of our country or the world some or all of these things may be taboo . . . . [D]on't assume that all areas are identical when it comes to taboos. . . . (Remember, our goal is acceptance, the basis of a grace state of mind.)

(from *The Grace Awakening*
by Charles Swindoll)

RESPONSE

Use these questions to share more deeply with each other.

7. What issues cause debates among Christians you know?

____

____

____

8. How can believers handle controversial issues in a way that builds up the church rather than harms it?

____

____

____

9. How can believers show love and acceptance to one another, in spite of differing opinions on certain issues?

____

____

____

PRAYER

We ask you, Father, to protect your church. Keep us from making our personal rights more important than the unity of your church. Keep us focused on the important things, the things that will build your kingdom. Give us the strength to love and accept one another. Bind us together through your Holy Spirit.

JOURNALING

Take a few moments to record your personal insights from this lesson.

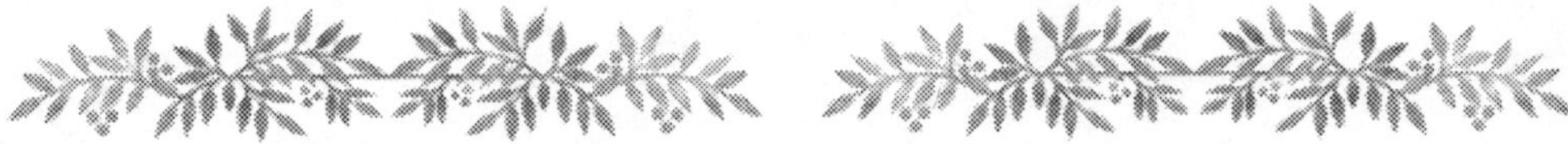

How can I be more sensitive to the beliefs of my Christian friends?

ADDITIONAL QUESTIONS

10. In your opinion, what are some issues that are not worth fighting over?

11. What beliefs are you not willing to compromise?

12. How can you avoid causing fellow believers to stumble in their faith?

For more Bible passages on accepting others, see Matthew 7:1–5; Romans 15:7; 1 Corinthians 4:5; Galatians 2:6; James 4:12.

To complete the book of Romans during this twelve-part study, read Romans 14:1–15:13.

ADDITIONAL THOUGHTS

LESSON TWELVE

LET IT SHINE

REFLECTION

Begin your study by sharing thoughts on this question.

1. How has the positive example of another believer encouraged you?

____

____

____

BIBLE READING

Read Romans 15:14–21 from the NCV or the NKJV.

NCV

14My brothers and sisters, I am sure that you
are full of goodness. I know that you have all
the knowledge you need and that you are able
to teach each other. 15But I have written to you
very openly about some things I wanted you to
remember. I did this because God gave me this
special gift: 16to be a minister of Christ Jesus to
those who are not Jews. I served God by teaching his Good News, so that the non-Jewish
people could be an offering that God would

NKJV

14Now I myself am confident concerning
you, my brethren, that you also are full of goodness, filled with all knowledge, able also to
admonish one another. 15Nevertheless, brethren, I have written more boldly to you on some
points, as reminding you, because of the grace
given to me by God, 16that I might be a minister of Jesus Christ to the Gentiles, ministering
the gospel of God, that the offering of the
Gentiles might be acceptable, sanctified by the

NCV

accept—an offering made holy by the Holy
Spirit.

17So I am proud of what I have done for God
in Christ Jesus. 18I will not talk about anything
except what Christ has done through me in
leading those who are not Jews to obey God.
They have obeyed God because of what I have
said and done, 19because of the power of mir-
acles and the great things they saw, and because of the power of the Holy Spirit. I preached
the Good News from Jerusalem all the way
around to Illyricum, and so I have finished that
part of my work. 20I always want to preach the
Good News in places where people have never
heard of Christ, because I do not want to build
on the work someone else has already started.
21But it is written in the Scriptures:

> "Those who were not told about him
> will see,
> and those who have not heard about him
> will understand."

NKJV

Holy Spirit. 17Therefore I have reason to glory
in Christ Jesus in the things which pertain
to God. 18For I will not dare to speak of any
of those things which Christ has not accomplished through me, in word and deed, to make
the Gentiles obedient— 19in mighty signs and
wonders, by the power of the Spirit of God,
so that from Jerusalem and round about to
Illyricum I have fully preached the gospel
of Christ. 20And so I have made it my aim to
preach the gospel, not where Christ was named,
lest I should build on another man's founda-
tion, 21but as it is written:

> "To whom He was not announced, they
> shall see;
> And those who have not heard shall under-
> stand."

DISCOVERY

Explore the Bible reading by discussing these questions.

2. What was the basis of Paul's confidence in the Christians in Rome?

____

____

____

3. List some of the things God had accomplished through Paul's life.

4. What has God accomplished through your life?

5. Why did Paul prefer not to minister where others had already ministered? Was this a wise decision?

6. What principles of evangelism from Paul's life can you apply in your life?

INSPIRATION

Here is an uplifting thought from the *Inspirational Study Bible.*

A few nights ago a peculiar thing happened.

An electrical storm caused a blackout in our neighborhood. When the lights went out, I felt my way through the darkness into the storage closet where we keep the candles for nights like this. . . . I took my match and lit four of them. . . .

I was turning to leave with the large candle in my hand when I heard a voice, "Now, hold it right there."

"Who said that?"

"I did." The voice was near my hand.

"Who are you? What are you?"

"I'm a candle."

I lifted up the candle to take a closer look. You won't believe what I saw. There was a tiny face in the wax . . . a moving, functioning, fleshlike face full of expression and life.

"Don't take me out of here!"

"What?"

"I said, Don't take me out of this room."

"What do you mean? I have to take you out. You're a candle. Your job is to give light. It's dark out there."

"But you can't take me out. I'm not ready," the candle explained with pleading eyes. "I need more preparation."

I couldn't believe my ears. "More preparation?"

"Yeah, I've decided I need to research this job of light-giving so I won't go out and make a bunch of mistakes. You'd be surprised how distorted the glow of an untrained candle can be. . . ."

"All right then," I said. "You're not the only candle on the shelf. I'll blow you out and take the others!"

But just as I got my cheeks full of air, I heard other voices.

"We aren't going either!"

. . . I turned around and looked at the three other candles. . . . "You are candles and your job is to light dark places!"

"Well, that may be what you think," said the candle on the far left. . . . "You may think we have to go, but I'm busy. . . . I'm meditating on the importance of light. It's really enlightening." . . .

"And you other two," I asked, "are you going to stay in here as well?"

A short, fat, purple candle with plump cheeks that reminded me of Santa Claus spoke up. "I'm waiting to get my life together. I'm not stable enough."

The last candle had a female voice, very pleasant to the ear. "I'd like to help," she explained, "but lighting the darkness is not my gift. . . . I'm a singer. I sing to other candles to encourage them to burn more brightly."

. . . She began a rendition of "This Little Light of Mine." . . . The other three joined in, filling the storage room with singing. . . . I took a step back and considered the absurdity of it all. Four perfectly healthy candles singing to each other about light but refusing to come out of the closet.

(from *God Came Near*
by Max Lucado)

RESPONSE

Use these questions to share more deeply with each other.

7. How does Paul's example inspire you to get more actively involved in evangelism?

8. What has hindered your witness for Christ?

9. How can you overcome that hindrance?

PRAYER

Father, forgive us for ignoring the lost; forgive us for selfishly enjoying the gift of your salvation, without sharing it with others; forgive us for the times we have kept our mouths shut, burying the truth of your Word, for fear of ridicule or rejection. Fill us with courage, Father. Use us as instruments of your mercy and grace extended to a world bound by sin.

JOURNALING

Take a few moments to record your personal insights from this lesson.

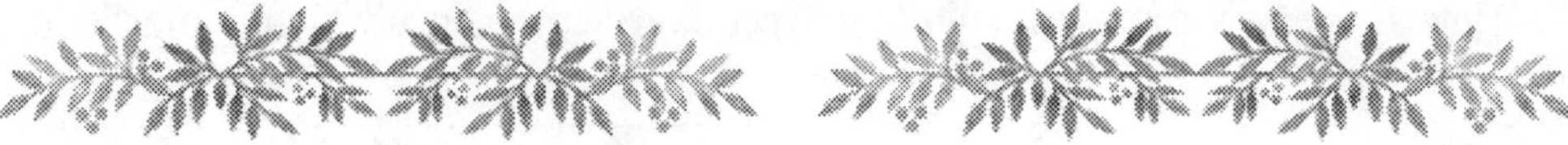

How well is this light of mine shining?

ADDITIONAL QUESTIONS

10. Are you reluctant to talk about God with others? How can you overcome that reluctance?

____

____

____

11. What are some creative ways of sharing the gospel?

____

____

____

12. Who shared the gospel message with you? How can you thank that person?

____

____

____

For more Bible passages on evangelism, see Matthew 5:13–16; 28:18–20; Acts 1:8; 2 Corinthians 2:14–17; 1 Thessalonians 2:8; 1 Peter 3:15,16.

To complete the book of Romans during this twelve-part study, read Romans 15:14–16:27.

ADDITIONAL THOUGHTS

LEADERS' NOTES

LESSON ONE

Question 2: God reveals himself to people in many ways. The revelation of God through creation is called general revelation (Psalm 19:1; Acts 14:17; Romans 1:20). God also reveals himself through the Bible (Psalm 19:8; Romans 1:16; 1 John 5:13); the Holy Spirit (John 14:26; 1 Corinthians 2:13); and the incarnation of Christ (John 12:49; 14:10). This is called special revelation.

Question 8: Some people don't understand how to establish a right relationship with God. Others have misconstrued ideas based on their own assumptions. This question will challenge the group to examine their own beliefs, lay aside any misconceptions, and acknowledge the truth of the gospel. Remind your group of Christ's words in John 14:6.

LESSON TWO

Question 8: This question will challenge the group to acknowledge the difference between having religion and having a relationship with Christ. You might follow up with this question: How can you determine whether you truly know Jesus?

Question 9: Hypocrisy is acting like something you are not or pretending to be religious when your heart is far from God. Jesus' teaching on the subject is recorded in Matthew 6:2–8; 7:1–6; 15:5–9; 23:1–36 and Luke 6:41, 42; 12:1, 2.

LESSON THREE

Question 3: God's plan of salvation is summarized in Romans 3:22–24. The law and the prophets told of God's plan long before Jesus came to earth. If you have time, ask someone in the group to read aloud Isaiah 52:13–53:12. If you don't have time, encourage group members to read this passage on their own.

You may need to explain some of the following terms during this study. (1) Justification refers to God's declaration that we are not guilty for our sins. (2) Redemption means that Jesus paid the penalty for our sins by dying on the cross. (3) Atonement refers to Christ's sacrifice on our behalf.

LESSON FOUR

This passage is better understood in light of Abraham's life story. Read these key passages to prepare yourself for the discussion: Genesis 12:1–4; 15:1–6; 22:1–18 and Galatians 3:6–9.

Question 2: Abraham was not saved because of his love for God, his good works, or his adherence to religious rituals. His faith made him right with God.

LESSON FIVE

Question 3: The results of sin are described in Ezra 9:6, 7; Psalm 66:18; Proverbs 23:29–35; Isaiah 1:4–7; 59:2; Hosea 5:5–7 and Matthew 13:15.

Question 4: The results of obedience to God are described in Exodus 19:5, 6; Deuteronomy 5:29; Proverbs 23:17, 18; Matthew 12:50; John 14:23; James 1:25 and 1 John 3:22–24.

Question 8: Encourage participants to read these verses about dealing with temptation: Matthew 26:41; 1 Corinthians 10:13; Galatians 6:1 and Hebrews 2:17, 18; 4:14–16.

LESSON SIX

Question 4: The Spirit of God gives people new life (John 6:63; 2 Corinthians 3:6); empowers believers for special tasks (Judges 3:10); helps believers worship (John 4:23–24); enables believers to spread the gospel (Matthew 10:19–20); and guides, teaches and convicts people (Luke 12:12; John 14:26; 16:7–13).

LESSON SEVEN

Question 6: Romans 10:14–15 emphasizes the importance of spreading the gospel message. It's tempting to assume that these verses were written to evangelists and pastors, but every believer is responsible to share the good news. See 2 Kings 7:9; Matthew 9:35–38; 28:18–20 and Acts 1:8.

Question 12: Ask group members to consider these questions: If you don't tell your neighbor about God, who will? What may happen if you don't share the gospel with your unsaved friends? How does God want you to become more involved in spreading the gospel message?

LESSON EIGHT

This study includes references to Old Testament passages. Elijah's appeal to God against Israel is recorded in 1 Kings 19:10–18. The prophet Isaiah's prediction that God would punish hard-hearted people is found in Isaiah 6:9–13. Romans 11:8 is based on Deuteronomy 29:4 and Isaiah 29:10. Verses 9 and 10 are taken from Psalm 69:22, 23.

LESSON NINE

Question 2: In Old Testament times, animals were offered as sacrifices to God to atone for the sins of the people. When Jesus died on the cross, he became the perfect sacrifice. He bore the penalty for our sin and offered us salvation through his blood. We show our gratitude by offering ourselves as living sacrifices to God.

Question 5: Paul compared the body of Christ to the human body to illustrate how believers should work together and support one another. Encourage participants to take time in the next few weeks to identify their spiritual gifts and determine how to use them for the encouragement of other Christians. Refer them to 1 Corinthians 12:12–31; 14:1–40 and Ephesians 4:1–16. If the group expresses interest in learning more about spiritual gifts, you could suggest this as the next topic of study.

LESSON TEN

Question 2: Loving others is not an option, something we can do when it is convenient or when others treat us well. Loving others is our responsibility. Our lives are indebted to Christ because of what he did for us on the cross. Although we can never repay him, we demonstrate our appreciation by showing God's love to others.

Question 6: Give group members time to think through what it means to "clothe yourself with the Lord Jesus" and how to apply it to daily life. It may help to read these passages: Galatians 3:26, 27; Ephesians 4:22–24; Colossians 3:9–17.

Question 8: The group can learn more about God's view of love by reading Jeremiah 31:3; John 3:16; 14:15; 16:27; Romans 5:8; 1 Corinthians 13:1–13; Ephesians 2:4, 5 and 1 John 3:1; 4:7–21. You may select several of these passages for group members to read aloud.

LESSON ELEVEN

Question 3: Paul emphasized the importance of unity among believers. Christians must carefully weigh the consequences of their actions and consider how their choices will impact fellow believers.

Question 4: This debate over eating food offered to idols may not seem relevant today. This question will help the group focus on the timeless truth of Romans 14:17. It is crucial that the group keeps this verse in mind as they move on to the next set of questions.

Questions 7, 8, and 9: If your group loves a good debate, encourage them to save their arguments about current controversial issues until after the study is completed. The goal of this study is not to resolve controversies but to learn how to build up and support other believers, even those who have different opinions.

LESSON TWELVE

Question 6: Other principles of evangelism are described in Matthew 9:37–38; 28:18–20; Acts 1:8; Romans 1:14–17; 2 Corinthians 4:1–6; and 1 Thessalonians 1:4–10.

Question 11: You can direct this question to individuals or to the group as a whole. Ask the group to consider how they could work together to help spread the gospel to those who haven't heard.

ADDITIONAL NOTES

ADDITIONAL NOTES

ADDITIONAL NOTES

ADDITIONAL NOTES

ADDITIONAL NOTES

ADDITIONAL NOTES

ADDITIONAL NOTES

ADDITIONAL NOTES

Acknowledgments

Brown, Joan W. *Day by Day with Billy Graham*, World Wide Publishers, copyright 1976.
Graham, Billy. *Peace with God*, copyright 1984, Word, Inc., Dallas, Texas.
Graham, Billy. *Unto the Hills*, copyright 1986, Word, Inc., Dallas, Texas.
Keller, Philip. *A Gardener Looks at the Fruits of the Spirit*, copyright 1986, Word, Inc., Dallas, Texas.
Lucado, Max. *God Came Near*, Questar Publishers, Multnomah Books, copyright 1987.
Lucado, Max. *In the Eye of the Storm*, copyright 1991, Word, Inc., Dallas, Texas.
Lucado, Max. *On the Anvil*, copyright 1985 by Max Lucado. Used by permission of Tyndale House Publishers, Inc. All rights reserved.
MacDonald, William. *Alone in Majesty*, copyright 1994 by Thomas Nelson, Nashville, Tennessee.
Swindoll, Charles. *The Grace Awakening*, copyright 1990, Word, Inc., Dallas, Texas.